Welcome to
30 days of gratitude.
A great way to start a new habit to improve your mindset.
Set aside a few minutes every day to focus on all the abundance you have in your life right now.

GRATITUDE ROCKS!
TODAY I AM SO GRATEFUL FOR...

DAY 1

GRATITUDE ROCKS!
TODAY I AM SO GRATEFUL FOR...

DAY 2

GRATITUDE ROCKS!
TODAY I AM SO GRATEFUL FOR...

DAY 3

GRATITUDE ROCKS!
TODAY I AM SO GRATEFUL FOR...

DAY 4

GRATITUDE ROCKS!
TODAY I AM SO GRATEFUL FOR...

DAY 5

GRATITUDE ROCKS!
TODAY I AM SO GRATEFUL FOR...

DAY 6

GRATITUDE ROCKS!
TODAY I AM SO GRATEFUL FOR...

DAY 7

GRATITUDE ROCKS!
TODAY I AM SO GRATEFUL FOR...

DAY 8

GRATITUDE ROCKS!
TODAY I AM SO GRATEFUL FOR...

DAY 9

GRATITUDE ROCKS!
TODAY I AM SO GRATEFUL FOR...

DAY 10

GRATITUDE ROCKS!
TODAY I AM SO GRATEFUL FOR...

DAY 11

GRATITUDE ROCKS!
TODAY I AM SO GRATEFUL FOR...

DAY 12

GRATITUDE ROCKS!
TODAY I AM SO GRATEFUL FOR...

DAY 13

GRATITUDE ROCKS!
TODAY I AM SO GRATEFUL FOR...

DAY 14

GRATITUDE ROCKS!
TODAY I AM SO GRATEFUL FOR...

DAY 15

GRATITUDE ROCKS!
TODAY I AM SO GRATEFUL FOR...

DAY 16

GRATITUDE ROCKS!
TODAY I AM SO GRATEFUL FOR...

DAY 17

GRATITUDE ROCKS!
TODAY I AM SO GRATEFUL FOR...

DAY 18

GRATITUDE ROCKS!
TODAY I AM SO GRATEFUL FOR...

DAY 19

GRATITUDE ROCKS!
TODAY I AM SO GRATEFUL FOR...

DAY 20

GRATITUDE ROCKS!
TODAY I AM SO GRATEFUL FOR...

DAY 21

GRATITUDE ROCKS!
TODAY I AM SO GRATEFUL FOR...

DAY 22

GRATITUDE ROCKS!
TODAY I AM SO GRATEFUL FOR...

DAY 23

GRATITUDE ROCKS!
TODAY I AM SO GRATEFUL FOR...

DAY 24

GRATITUDE ROCKS!
TODAY I AM SO GRATEFUL FOR...

DAY 25

GRATITUDE ROCKS!
TODAY I AM SO GRATEFUL FOR...

DAY 26

GRATITUDE ROCKS!
TODAY I AM SO GRATEFUL FOR...

DAY 27

GRATITUDE ROCKS!
TODAY I AM SO GRATEFUL FOR...

DAY 28

GRATITUDE ROCKS!
TODAY I AM SO GRATEFUL FOR...

DAY 29

GRATITUDE ROCKS!
TODAY I AM SO GRATEFUL FOR...

DAY 30

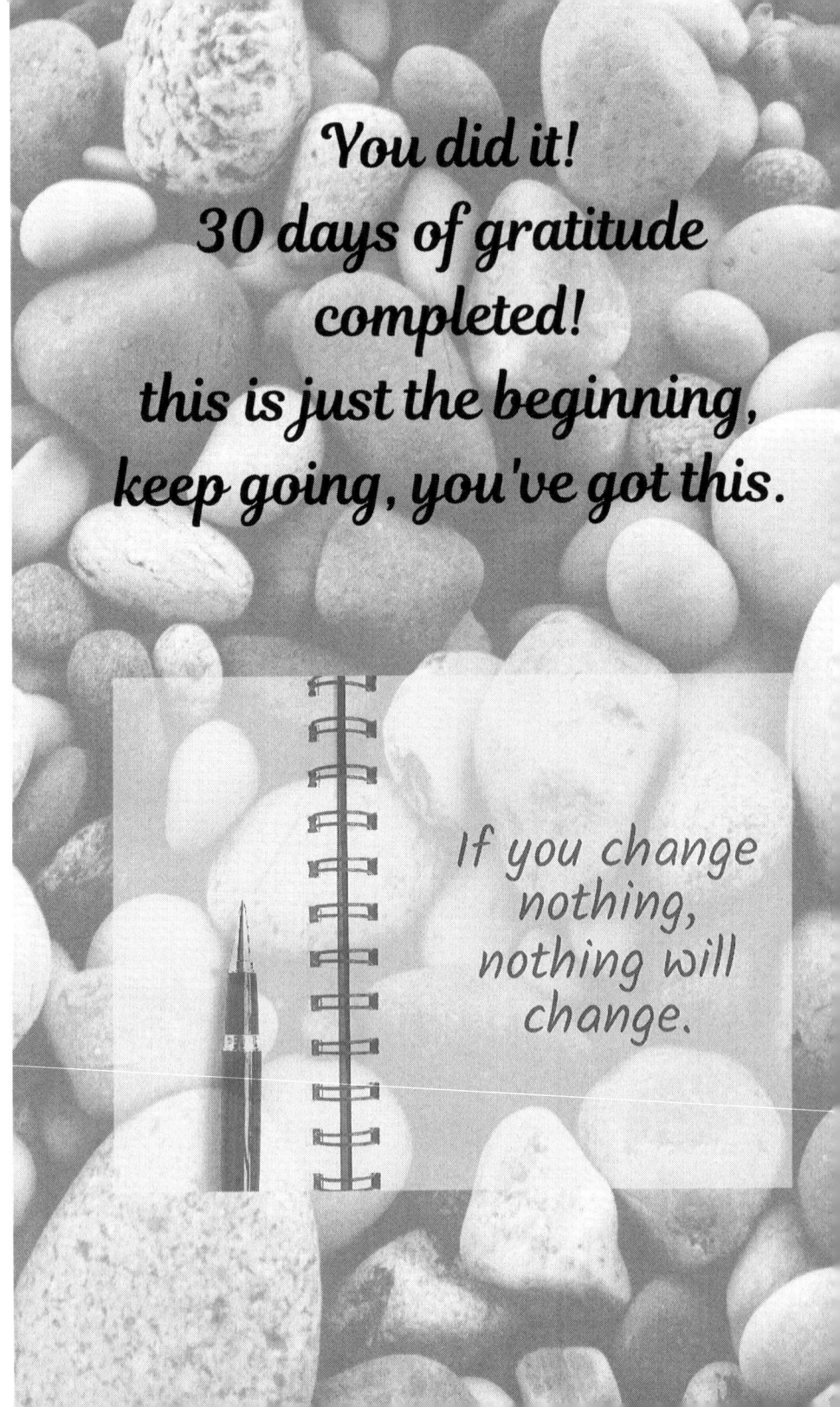

Printed in Great Britain
by Amazon